The Sword and The Sickle

A Prayer Warrior's Guide to Praying the Scriptures

By
Rev. Juli E. Jasinski

For more information on Rev. Juli E. Jasinski's books contact her directly at:

Juli E. Jasinski
Cell: 603 557-2071

Email: Pwrxtrem2@aol.com

Follow me on Facebook

Dedication

To my son, Andrew who inspired me by your perseverance
when the odds were against you

&

To all the Prayer Warriors who strive for more

So shall my word be
That goes forth out of my mouth:
It shall not return unto me void, but it shall accomplish
that which I please, and it shall prosper in the thing for
which I sent it.
Isaiah 55:11

Introduction

Nothing will ever take the place of a man or a woman who humble them self and spend time in prayer. There are several books written to stir you to pray, and, others tell of the history of people who changed their world through a life of prayer yet, reading these books will never replace the very act of getting down on your knees and talking to God.

From time to time we all could admit that we need something to change in our prayer life. We must endeavor to keep it from growing cold. Have you ever gone through a phase where you just couldn't seem to get a grip on the Spirit? Didn't you feel like the heavens were brass?

And even though your heart was filled with desire for God to move in the life of others your prayers seemed to only reach the ceiling and fall dead. Perhaps even now you've been feeling a little dry and a bit bored during your own personal prayer time. It may be because you're lacking that life-giving power and vigor that one needs to have an effective prayer life?

Praying the Word of God is a powerful tool to bring about the desired change in your life, your family and even your community. If you learn to tank up on God's Word, and use it during your prayer time, you'll see amazing things happen in your prayer life and in the world around you.

Every Christian person who is on fire for God usually burns with desire to win some destitute soul to Jesus. The Lord cares deeply for them, we must tell them so. But, how can we win this war for the lost if our prayers are empty words laced with vain repetitions? Do we offer up prayers without fuel while the devil scuffs at our parody? How can we be victorious warriors with no power to fight? Mere verbiage will not get the job done. One wonders if God looks in dismay at us over the balcony of heaven. Jesus called these "vain repetitions" (Matthew 6:7).

The most precious commodity of mankind is our time. If we don't invest it wisely by sacrificing it to the Lord, then all the prayer clocks, prayer systems and prayer objectives lay dormant and are rendered useless to the child of God. Our walk with God is in jeopardy of being dull and mundane.

Some Christians wish to have an audience with the Lord but do not want to surrender a few extra minutes to get the Spirit moving on the inside of our hearts. And then there are some people who aren't sure _how_ to approach Him that will be pleasing to God. (*Perhaps this is your case*).

Maybe at times, you feel the heavens are brass and the earth is hard as steel (Deut. 28:23). You desperately hope He's listening but aren't sure if He is, and, you only have a few minutes to try to reach Him before you blast off to the list of things you need to get done.

Prayer is more than wishful thinking. You need more than a hit and miss approach to get the job done. Hebrews 11:6 assures us that, "...***He is a rewarder of them that diligently seek him.***"

We must approach the throne of grace earnestly and sincerely. It must be more than a 3-sentence invocation over your meals or a good-night benediction. Every one of His children must choose to humbly go into his or her prayer closet and begin.

Where exactly do we start? How do we get our prayers answered? What are some of the key elements to achieve successful prayer time? First of all, it requires a setting your mind _to_ pray.

You need plenty of willingness to commit to the life-long endeavor. And, a boat load of self-discipline to finish the task. It's more than a "task," it's a divine appointment. It's a relationship connection that leads to a divine romance.

One must realize there are opposing forces at work to stop you from getting to God. Thus, the greatest battle in a fruitful prayer life is "*just doing it.*" And watch out, the flesh will fight you every step of the way.

The brain will wonder, and the knees will ache and, undoubtedly, the phone will ring. Oft times, the spirit is willing but the flesh is weak. It's imperative that the spirit-man rise and demand you spend time in prayer.

If you press on through the distractions, you will happily find God...Acts 17:27, ***"That they should seek the Lord, if haply they might feel after him, and find him, though he be not far from every one of us."***

In time, you will find the Lord standing there waiting for you on the other side. Crossing the bridge of distractions is where you'll find the peace, joy, and love of God.

After a few years of my Holy Ghost conversion, my regular prayer life began to be established. I stumbled upon (*or God led me to*) a great secret in praying effectively (*it was quite easy*). It's the art of bringing God's Word into your prayer time.

One lady said you've got to "work the Word!" I believe she is saying that we must put the Word of God into action by releasing it in prayer.

I made an interesting discovery a few years back on my first trip to Israel. One day after a tour, our group went to the gift shops. I purchased a Jewish prayer book. To my surprise, it didn't contain a religious man's wordy prayers but the entire Book of Psalms.

I learned later that during the time of prayer at the Wailing Wall, the Jews used this book (*and others*) to pray God's Word directly back to Him (*brilliant idea*).

Although it was a new concept to me, it was not a new one to them for they have been praying this way for centuries.

Consequently, I decided to try it for myself. The results were overwhelming. I found that using God's Word as a prayer book helped me reap benefits beyond measure.

A few benefits worth mentioning here now are: 1) it helps to keep you focused in prayer, and 2) assists you to memorize the Scriptures. And, the most significant reward is…3) you get instant results.

God Almighty stops by and listens. His heavenly hosts are on standby ready to be dispatched. When you pray God's Word back to Him, you feel the rush of Holy Ghost surge thru your spirit. His word is like crystal clean water pouring thru your mind; cleaning it ever so gently.

The lesson to learn here is, in praying God's Word you are speaking God's language. Let's ponder this a moment. He wrote the Book. You are speaking His very own words back to Him. You are communicating to Him on the same proverbial "wave length."

I received a greater understanding of this concept when I went on a road trip to Mexico. I knew a few phases in Spanish and spoke them to the church folks. Their eyes just lit up. I could see that they were delighted I could communicate to them in their own native tongue. The feeling was mutual.

They desired to communicate to me as I did with them. Like my newly acquired Mexican friends who were pleased when I spoke in their language, God is pleased when we speak His language. Consequently, when we do, God is willing to talk back to us.

Another way to think about it is like this: God's Word in our mouth is like a combustion engine. A flame is ignited then forces all the integral parts to work. This force moves the component over a distance. God's Word sets our heart on fire and fuels us to pray with fervor so that we may be able to complete His purposes in our lives.

The Lord said through the prophet Jeremiah, *"I will make my words in your mouth fire"* (5:14). Communicating to God in His own language will burn away any barriers. It clears the path to get to Him. *"The path of the righteous is level; You clear a straight path for the righteous"* (Isa 26:7) (Holman).

The Word of God clears the path for us like the proverbial snowplow man. Here in New England, it's imperative that we have this guy push away the snow and clear us a path so that we can get out to the driveway on a wintry day.

As we speak God's Word, we hurl the Sword of the Spirit into the Heavenlies to do a work for us. When we have the Sword in our mouth, we obtain the mighty power to defeat the enemy from all hindrances.

Dick Eastman writes in his book, *The Hour that Changes the World,* "to neglect God's Word [in our prayer time] is to neglect God's power."[1] The Bible is like no other book in the world. One cannot explain it fully but there is something very supernatural when quoting the Word of God (especially in prayer).

The Scriptures come to life from off the cold pages of that sacred Book. They are alive on their own but need to be activated. Quoting God's Word is the releasing of God's power to accomplish what He pleases.

We can attest that the Word of God is the **power** of God. The Lord declares in Isaiah 55:11, *"So shall my word be that goes forth out of my mouth: it shall not return unto me void, but it shall accomplish that which I please, and it shall prosper in the thing for which I sent it."*

"I will first fight prayer's battles in the prayer room," says renowned prayer warrior, Vesta Mangun of Alexandria Louisiana. She continues, *"Throughout the day I will then collect the spoils."* Sis Mangun indicates that the battle is primarily in prayer room. This is the place where we engage in spiritual warfare. As we stand fully dressed in the Armor of God, we hurl the Sword of the Spirit to destroy the enemy's schemes and proclaim God's promises.

---

[1] Dick Eastman, *The Hour That Changes The World*, (Baker Book House Company, 1978) 55.

When we remain faithful to a habit of prayer (commonly known as one's prayer life), we become mighty instruments in the hands of God. Not only does Sister Mangun refer to this practice as her prayer life, but, as "a life of prayer."

Sis Mangun is a woman who has endeavored to give her whole life to prayer. She declares that throughout the day one will reap the benefits of praying fervently by collecting the spoils to advance the Kingdom of God.

Jesus said, *"...the words that I speak unto you, they are spirit, and they are life,"* (John 6:63). The very words of the Lord are mighty and full of life ready to go to work for us. He wants to work with us, in us and through us (Eph. 4:5). We must simply strike the match.

It's the privilege of every believer to obtain this unique power which comes from directly praying the Word of God. You must experience it for yourself.

Most of us in the church can sense the pressure that time is running out like the proverbial sands in an hour glass...sinners feel it too. Humanity's clock is ticking closer to the soon coming of the Lord.

One can't help but feel the urgency of the hour which demands a renewed strength and power. You probably feel it, I know I do. But what is the church doing about it as a whole?

It's no secret that church attendance has dropped in many churches. Perhaps it reflects the absence of dynamic praying that is so easy to obtain. Where are God's prayer warriors?

Jesus said to His disciples that no man knows what day or hour when He is going to come back for His bride (Matt. 24:36). It won't be long now 'til this life will be over.

There is an uneasy feeling that we are playing a losing game of beat the clock. Therefore, it is important that we pray more effectively and not just beat the air with empty powerless words.

Christianity has fallen asleep spiritually. This may be the plight of all denominations. All the while, men and women in the world are remaining dead in trespasses and sins. They are the living dead and the churches are sleep walkers.

The heart of desire has stopped beating with passion. The Church prayer rooms have been replaced by offices. It's as though there is a buildup of plaque in the arteries of smooth-running prayer. This has been brought on by the busyness and cares of this life.

Blood clots of lethargy have blocked the main arteries that flow to the heart of Jesus. As an EMT would work feverishly on a victim that has a cardiac arrest so must our prayer warriors become fervent to get the flow of oxygen to the heart of the Church. It must pump again with a passion for prayer.

We need the Holy Ghost to place the paddles of conviction on our heart and once again, shock us, revive us, and renew us to the place we first believed. Lord, bring us back to life! Can you just hear the sirens? Can you feel the paddles on your soul?

Remember the joy we felt when we first came to Jesus. Remember how the enemy lost his grip on us when we repented and gave our life over to Jesus. We felt so free. No more bondage, no more chains.

We can't let that freedom die. As Spirit-filled Christians we must learn how to use the Sword of Spirit. We have the potential to do some serious damage to the devil's debauched empire and restore victory to God's Kingdom.

The enemy is growing ever-so angry knowing his time is short (Rev. 12:12) and seeks to take back territory he once owned. However, where sin abounds, grace abounds much more (Rom.5:20).

We are his greatest threat. The Word of God is our best defense. You and I have too many lost ones to let them slip into a burning hell. We must be fervent, and steadfast to conquer the devil and all his demons. And by using the Word of God in prayer time, it will help us keep our eye on the goal.

Learning how to use God's Word makes us stronger in God and builds our faith. In her book, *The Prayer Journey,* Fredi Trammell states, "Scripture becomes an unseen sword to enable us to fend off the cruelest of enemies."[2]

The Lord spoke to her in a time when she was overwhelmingly concerned due to a physical condition of her son. The Lord said to her, "When you behold any opposition carnal vision, fear will immediately paralyze your faith."

---

[2] Fredi Trammell, *The Prayer Journey*, (Harmony Ministries, 1991) 77.

It is important to note that God's Spirit will destroy our fear for the Bible declares, *"For God hath not given us the spirit of fear; but of power, and of love, and of a sound mind"* (2 Tim. 1:7).

Reminding her readers, Trammell says that Jesus did attest that, *"If ye abide in me and MY WORDS ABIDE IN YOU, ye shall ask what ye will, and it shall be done unto you"* (John 15:7).

She makes a convincing point that there can be no greater or more powerful method of prayer than that of praying directly from God's Word. Jesus was the best example of this and King David also.[3] We prayer warriors should follow their examples.

His Word must abide in us, be a part of us, and dominant a large part of our prayer life. This is a good habit to get into especially for a new believer's walk with God. This will teach them how and what to pray.

Thus, as the words of the Lord begin to abide in us, our mind will be flooded with scriptures, our soul will be nurtured, and the inner man strengthened. Consequently, His Spirit will make us armed and dangerous to ward off attacks and ambushes of the devil.

The results: our on-going deliberate acts in prayer will snuff out anything that hinders us from obtaining the victory. We can win souls for Jesus Christ just by praying the Word.

---

[3] Ibid.

11

This must be a repetitious action however. A single blow of a sledge hammer cannot eradicate an unwanted concrete slab. One must continue to strike it until it breaks up in to small removable pieces. Our persistent unrelenting prayers will break up the fallow ground. Each striking blow will give us strength to abide in His Word.

Remember Jesus told us in Luke 10:19, *"Behold, I give unto you <u>power</u> to tread on serpents and scorpions, and over all the <u>power</u> of the enemy: and nothing shall by any means hurt you."* The word power is used twice in this scripture and has two different meanings.

The first power is rendered "authority." The second power, "power of the enemy" simply means force, or miraculous power. In most cases the devil will manifest him as being forceful and showing of an extraordinary power.

For example: The devil tried to show off when he showed up in the book of Act 19:13. The seven sons of Sceva took it upon themselves to cast out evil spirits.

They had no authority to do so. So, the spirits spoke back, beat them boys and prevailed against them. The boys eventually ran out of the house naked and wounded. *(That must have been quite a sight)*

The devil showed what he could do to someone not covered by the blood of Jesus. Thus, the devil has power but his is limited. Keep that in mind and you'll always prevail.

It is the hope of the author that you, *"be strong in the Lord, and in the power of his might"* (Eph. 6:10). As you gain strength anew, may you become as the heroes of faith in Hebrew 11:34, *"out of weakness were made strong, became valiant in war, turned to flight the armies of foreigners."*

May you be able to *"hear what the Spirit said to the churches"* (Rev. 2:7). And, *"knowing therefore the terror of the Lord,"* I pray you may be able to *"persuade men"* to come to Jesus (2 Cor.5:11) and try to *"save others by snatching them from the fire"* (Jude 23) NIV.

Jesus told His disciples to *"look up, and lift up your heads; for your redemption draweth nigh"* (Luke 21:28). We must work *"while it is day: the night cometh, when no man can work"* (John 9:4). And just as John the Revelator said, *"Even so, come Lord Jesus"* (Rev. 22:20).

It is the purpose of this book to guide you the reader into a power-filled, soul-winning experience. This book is a tool intended to get you started in praying God's Word. **It's a prayer warrior's guide to praying the scriptures.**

Let's begin our prevailing journey with The Sword and the Sickle

The Sword & The Sickle

༶

Write the vision, and make it
Plain upon tables,
That he may run that readeth it.
For the vision is yet for an appointed time.
Habakkuk 2:2-3

Chapter ONE

THE VISION

Soon after my husband and I got married, we committed ourselves to go to our church's early Morning Prayer meeting at 6AM. One day during prayer while I was praying and rebuking the devil from my lost loved ones, the Lord showed me a vision. It came so suddenly.

He showed me that in one hand I held a Sword, and in the other, I had a Sickle. The impression was so strong as if the wooden handles were literally in my hands. I was stirred thinking, "what could this mean?" I saw myself swinging these objects back and forth like a harvest worker on a hot summer day.

Shortly thereafter, the Lord gave me the interpretation. He showed me that the Sword represented the scriptures I quoted to fight <u>against</u> the enemy while the Sickle represented the scriptures, I used to <u>reap</u> the souls that were ripe for harvest. These people lived throughout my city.

I realized then that this is how the Lord saw me when I was praying in this manner. The Sword and the Sickle were cutting through into the spiritual realm.

Up to this point, all I knew was that the Sword of Spirit was a part of the armor of God (Eph. 6:17). But the sickle, I had no idea being a city girl. I wondered what the sickle tool was used for.

Unbeknownst to me, these items were being used during my prayer time to cut away spirits. I later learned how that the Sword and the Sickle were going to be instrumental in praying for the revival of souls coming into my church.

There is one book I read prior to me receiving the vision. It was called, *The Believer's Authority* written by Kenneth Hagin.

I discovered a key point about the workings of the Sword of the Spirit. He pointed out that it was an <u>offensive weapon</u> to be used as a prayer to be prayed back to God.

For example, Hagin showed his readers that in Ephesians 1:16-20 and 3:14-20, these passages were not only prayers the apostle Paul prayed for the church in Ephesus, <u>but were prayers that we modern day saints of God could pray for ourselves daily.</u> Hagin called these "Spirit-anointed prayers."[4]

Let's look at these scriptures:

Ephesians 1:16-20

"Cease not to give thanks for you, making mention of you in my prayers; That the God of our Lord Jesus Christ, the Father of glory, may give unto you the spirit of wisdom and revelation in the knowledge of him: The eyes of your understanding being enlightened; that ye may know what is the hope of his calling, and what the riches of the glory of his inheritance in the saints, And what is the exceeding greatness of his power to us-ward who believe, according to the working of his mighty power, Which he wrought in Christ, when he raised him from the dead, and set him at his own right hand in the heavenly places,"

Ephesians 3:14-21

---

[1] Kenneth E. Hagin, *The Believer's Authority*, (Faith Library Publications 1984) 1.

"For this cause I bow my knees unto the Father of our Lord Jesus Christ, of whom the whole family in heaven and earth is named, That he would grant you, according to the riches of his glory, to be strengthened with might by his Spirit in the inner man; That Christ may dwell in your hearts by faith; that ye, being rooted and grounded in love, May be able to comprehend with all saints what is the breadth, and length, and depth, and height; And to know the love of Christ, which passeth knowledge, that ye might be filled with all the fullness of God. Now unto him that is able to do exceeding abundantly above all that we ask or think, according to the power that worketh in us."

Hagin encouraged his readers that in order to put these scriptures into <u>action</u> you must put them in the "first person singular" form. These pronouns are: I, me, and mine.

For example, in verse 18, "*...The eyes of your understanding being enlightened; that ye may know what is the hope of his calling...*" he suggests to quote it like this instead, *...The eyes of **my** understanding being enlightened; that **I** may know what is the hope of his calling,*" By doing so, we can make the scriptures become our own personal prayers.[5]

---

[2]Ibid, 2

After I began to apply this principle to my prayers, I felt the power of the Holy Ghost transform my prayer life. Almost immediately I saw results. And it's only because I prayed these two passages of scriptures using the first-person singular pronouns. It was amazing to me.

My prayers move with an ebullience of their own. Instead of droning on and on wearily, the Holy Ghost flooded my soul with joy (Psalms 16:11).

Months later, more light was shed on the subject when I went to a woman's conference in San Francisco. One of the speakers taught on this very same subject. She explained how that praying the scriptures could change your life forever. That it did.

I listened to her testimony of how God showed her the power in praying scriptures. I felt a conformation deep in my spirit that the Lord wanted me to continue in this vein of praying.

She told the audience about the astonishing results in her own prayer life. In a few short six weeks, her family made a great spiritual turn around all because of praying the Word of God. I want that, I thought.

I've got to go deeper in God. I bought her book and tape series, *"How to Pray for Your Loved Ones."* The author, Kathy Casto, taught her readers how to pray the Word of God over the people that we cared about in our life.

She mentioned for us to not only to pray the Word of God over yourself, but over your spouse, your children, your family, your pastor, your church, finances, and personal issues; over virtually everything.

That's an excellent idea. Casto insistently stated that praying the Word of God is praying the "will of God."[6] I was so excited to get started on my new found way of praying.

Ever since I've heard about it at the conference back in 1992, it's become my primary method of praying. It's anchored my prayer life and kept me focused for nearly 25 years.

As time passed and I got established in this new prayer routine, the Lord began to lead me further and further into His Word. I started with the two scriptures, then adding more to my list. I added more and more each week using her book as an example. It wasn't too long; I had worn her book out.

God's Word ignited my heart a blaze right in front of my eyes. His Word took on a life of Its own. He wanted me to continue to search out even more scriptures. Every time I read the Bible; scriptures jumped out at me like popcorn.

Suddenly, the eyes of my understanding opened to the fact that the Bible is more than just a book of holy stories; it is a complete prayer manual for us to use during our devotions.

From time to time however, doubt would press my mind. I wondered why God would want His children to pray His Word anyway. Was there something to gain by doing so? Would this really make a difference in one's life?

---

[3]Kathy Casto, *How to Pray for Your Loved Ones*, (Hisway Publications 1989) 22

The answer is simply this: **praying the Word of God** moves the Lord more readily into action. We pray, He answers. He tells His angels to do a work for His children (Hebrew 1:14).

We are solely His holy vessels endeavoring to get the prayer wheels turning. We are His people mandated with the responsibility to get His will accomplished.

But this vehicle only moves with supplication from His people to drive it; without such, His plans and purposes lay dormant in the earth.

God wants to work together with us. It's a fact that we must acknowledge. He knows what He is doing and knows what He needs to get accomplished. Think of it as a joint venture or a partnership between us and the Lord.

The Bible states that God's Word is a burning fire, a hammer, a lamp, and a light, (Jeremiah 23:29, Psalms 11:105). Our job is to simply hurl this masterpiece out there into the Heavenlies so that it can accomplish what God desires for it to do.

In the book of Isaiah chapter 55:11, *"So shall my word be that goeth forth out of my mouth: it shall not return unto me void, but it shall accomplish that which I please, and it shall prosper in the thing whereto I sent it."* Once God's Word is launched, the first place it lands is straight into the heart.

In the book of Hebrews 4:11 it says, *"For the word of God is quick [original Greek renders it:* **living**]*, and powerful [original Greek:* **active**]*, and sharper than any two-edged sword, piercing even to the dividing asunder of soul and spirit, and of the joints and marrow, and is a discerner of the thoughts and intents of the heart."*

God's Word is not old or archaic; it's alive. It is not inept or benign but dynamic and prevailing. No other book can match this one.

It reaches into the inner secrets of man's heart, mind, and soul to discern the thoughts and intents thereof. God can see us as if we are standing naked, unable to hide behind excuse or pretense.

The Bible indicates that by it (the Word of God), we are washed *"of water by the word"* (Eph. 5:26) and made clean. The Lord is aware of what's going on inside of us.

He knows yet desires that our thoughts first be purified from this world's influence. For us to *bow down* and *pray,* the carnal mind will attempt to squirm its way out of doing it.

It's important to be aware that our Holy God intently scrutinizes us (1 John 3:20). Thus, we must be willing to carefully examine our own life. We need to search our heart to see if there is any wicked way in us (Psa. 139:24).

You and I need to be washed before we approach His throne, but it can only be done by the cleansing of our mind by the Word of God.

Putting it plainly, His children need to take a good spiritual bath—and this is only done by soaking in the Word of God. A person who is a successful prayer warrior is a person whose heart is pure. And, the results of living right will produce an incredible life filled with effective prayers.

Once we are committed to pray, we are faced with the daunting reality that human words are somewhat vague. We run out of something to say (*or pray*) rather quickly.

And, because a man's or woman's physical power is limited, and our vocal cords sometimes get strained by speaking in tongues excessively, **praying the Word of God** advances us to a new level that takes flight and gets the job done.

It becomes a living catalyst to revive a fatigued prayer routine. Indeed, it's that jolt of energy like the proverbial monster drink to wake up the sleepy soul. Hence, it becomes the most powerful weapon in a prayer warrior's arsenal. We are the archer; God is the Invisible Hand that guides the arrow of the Scriptures to hit the bull's eye target.

"God wants us to believe His Word," Former First Lady Joy Haney of UPCI states, *"He wants us to live in His Word. His Word must dominate our minds. His Word causes us to speak faith before we see it done. We must [first] see it, speak it, and believe it!"*[7]

---

[4]*Praying the Word Effectively,* (Word Aflame Press, 2004) 10.

In order to use it [the Word of God], we must quote it, pray it, and hurl it out there into the Heavenlies. And let it do its perfect work.

One preacher said, *"Let us marinate our minds with God's Word."* His statement makes me think of chicken soaking in teriyaki sauce for days before a family BBQ. The chicken soaks in the sweetness of the marinate sauce and favors that meat.

God's Word causes our very thoughts to be sweet and focused on Him and His fullness.

As my prayer routine grew, praying the scriptures became a delightful passion and admittedly, a private obsession. The Lord led me to dig out more and more verses.

This helped me to pray more specifically for my lost loved ones and the city which our church was in.

One day I counted nearly 150 scriptures that I quoted in my prayer time. My mouth was dry, my body weary but I felt super charged in the Lord. The Holy Ghost gave me a surge of strength to persevere.

Here is the breakdown: I prayed 51 scriptures over myself, 31 for my husband and 25 over my son. There were 41 additional ones that I prayed for over my city and for soul winning purposes.

Later, I modified this prayer routine when it became bombastic. I began focusing on praying for one group at a time per day. For example: I would pray for myself on one day, and on another day for my husband and my son, and the other days for lost loved ones or special needs and others for my church family and for my city.

On Fridays however, I reserved that day to just thank Jesus for things in my life...last I counted it was 315 things!

My heart's greatest desire and deepest burden is to be an effective soul winner. I know this is God's will not only for me, but for all His Church.

There is a harvest of souls that He has ready to give us. But, does His church really believe that? Are we aware of the cry of the lost? Is the church ready to act on His great commission? Are we truly an outreach-minded people?

If all the churches in the USA were Jesus Name Apostolics, would we still be getting the job done? Could we really reach the 323 million people in our country or the 7.5 billion worldwide?

One may wonder what it takes to win a soul for Jesus anyway. The secret to winning someone is to daily use the Word of God in prayer. It's like a short cut to success.

Winning a soul is easier when you have prayed the Word directly for them. When you pray for them, you speak it directly into their life and spirit. Suddenly, you develop a deeper love for these people. And most likely, you will have a new found love for souls in general.

You will find it easier to quote scriptures when you are talking to people about the Bible because you searched out the scriptures to use them as prayers. For me I would think, *"Hey, this scripture would fit my mother, and this one for my brother and this one fit perfect to pray over my pastor and his family,"* etc.

Often, as I went about my business in town, I would see someone I know and think, *"Hey friend, I called out your name to God for you."* Sometimes, if the Lord led me, I'd tell them, and other times, I'd smile big and say it under my breath.

There are numerous soul-winning scriptures in the Bible that one could pray to tear down strongholds and rescue sinners.

If you are willing to dig them out to use for your own prayer purpose, you will become an apprentice of God's Word. One could never exhaust this divine resource; indeed, you'll be the one to wear out first.

All the while, there is no greater blessing then when you bring in the sheaves. What a joy when you have a hand in plucking sinners out of the fire.

Quoting the Word of God is the swinging of that Sickle as the Lord showed me in the vision. When people come to the Lord, there will be great rejoicing like the Psalmist David said, **"He that goeth forth and weepeth, bearing precious seed, shall doubtless come again with rejoicing bringing his sheaves with him"** (Psa. 126:6).

Jesus is our prime example of working the Word. Recall when He was tempted by the devil in the desert. He used the Word of God the fight back when He was confronted. He quoted the Word of God three times and won the victory each time. The devil couldn't stand it anymore and left.

We must use God's Word to command Satan to give up and swing those Holy Scriptures to cut like a sword severing the head of the wicked ones' influence. It is a sure method for triumph.

The enemy can't stand it, and for that matter, can't withstand us when we use scripture against him in Jesus Name. He cringes to the floor when he sees a Jesus-Name-Scripture-hurling prayer warrior taking back what he stole from us.

That kind of praying is sure to keep him in his place, bound by the blood of Jesus. Oh, how sweet the victory! (The devil doesn't want you to know that).

Our Lord left us with only one prayer request, *"Pray ye therefore the Lord of the harvest, that he will send forth laborers into his harvest"* (Matt. 9:380). And because the Lord is *"...not willing that any should perish, but that all should come to repentance"* (2 Peter 3:9), we must be diligent in reaching the lost and teaching them about salvation.

The Bible says in the next verse of 2 Peter that *"...the day of the Lord will come as a thief in the night,"* (vs. 10) we need to *"be ready always to give an answer to every man that asketh you a reason of the hope"* (1 Peter 3:15) and endeavor to reach the lost.

The Sword & The Sickle

❦

Blessed be the LORD my strength,
Who teaches my hands to war
And my fingers to fight
Psalms 144:1

Chapter TWO

PREPARATION FOR BATTLE

Every soldier must prepare himself mentally and physically before he engages in combat. The Army, the Navy or whichever branch of service it is, they all train their recruits for combat. Wouldn't it be foolish to take a raw recruit and thrust him into battle without some kind of training?

The Navy Seals have the most rigorous training to date. The novice goes in green and comes out a fighting machine; a burly bruising piece of work. He is educated proficiently and ready to engage in whatever conflict lays ahead. He has earned his title by enduring the rigors of training, scrutiny, and implementation.

So, it is the same with the Christian's personal prayer life. We must buckle down and learn the disciplines of an effective prayer warrior. In order to obtain our victories, we must be willing to do what it takes to get the job done.

Our goal is to win the lost for the Kingdom of God and turn our cities upside down as they did in the Book of Acts (17:6). No instruction or training is ever a waste of our time.

Our conquest, however, is won on our knees. We must stay on task and overcome all obstacles. Persistent prevailing prayer will always win out in the end, (*"The effectual fervent prayer of a righteous man avails much"* James 5:16).

Yet, the opposite principle is true. When we are slothful not shaking our self to pray...or when we refuse the invitation of the Lord to enter in our prayer closet...or when we decline the promptings of the Holy Ghost to go through the boot camp of prayer, we will inevitably experience defeat and suffer great losses.

First Samuel 12:23 declares, *"God forbid that I should sin against the LORD in ceasing to pray..."* By this careless negligent behavior, many believers end up back in the strongholds of the enemy. They nonchalantly sit in sin's prison of omission. Their heart grows cold towards the Lord.

As the civilian who is willing to enlist himself for the service of our country, we too, must enlist in a regiment of prayer-training. Our primary task at hand is disciplining our mind to pray prayer's battles. It can't be a *"now, lay me down to sleep"* kind of prayer.

Knowledge, training, and application in effective praying is the necessary groundwork to guarantee success. It is in prayer that the war rages, but it is also in prayer that our triumph is secured.

<u>LEARNING TO PRAY FOR YOURSELF</u>

Therefore, the first order of business is to PRAY FOR OURSELF; when we do, the mighty hand of God surrounds us with the fire of His Spirit. The book of Zechariah, chapter two verse five states, *"For I, says the LORD, will be unto her a wall of fire round about, and will be the glory in the midst of her."* His wall of fire will supply us with the strength to fight.

Some people may find it difficult to pray for their selves; it may be that they are ignorant of its necessity. We must pray for our self continually.

Let me state the obvious, no one knows <u>you</u> like you know yourself. And, because we know our self best, we can pray unashamedly before the Lord. And yes, it takes brutal honesty. (*"Behold, you desire truth in the inward parts: and in the hidden part* [secret heart] *you shall make me to know wisdom"* Psalms 51: 6).

Every saint of God struggles with some life issue. Everyone is fighting a battle. We need the Lord's help to overcome it. Then our honesty will clear a path to stand in the presence of the Lord.

The Psalmist David prayed to God to teach his hands to war and his fingers to fight (Psalms 144:1). Though this king of Israel was engaging in physical war he also needed strength for his spiritual battles. We too, must pray for the Lord to teach our hands to fight, no not physically, but to instruct us in what to say when we are praying.

We don't want to waste time using words that just beat the air. The best way to start praying for your self is to use a few familiar scriptures like "The Lord's Prayer" in Matthew 6:9-13. In time, the Lord will lead you to more specific scriptures that apply to your various needs.

The book of Psalms is loaded with self-revealing prayers. Many chapters speak of the conflict between David and his enemies. Other Psalms express the personal war deep within his heart that he was struggling with. The king was not afraid to disclose his inner feelings. As a man of war, and a man of prayer, he poured out his soul before the Lord. He was an excellent example of a person who unabashedly emptied his heart and allowed God to minister to him.

David stood in a place of surrender. We too, must come to this hallowed spot; for it is the place where we make ourselves vulnerable and transparent before the Lord. David cried out "*Search me, O God*" (Psa. 139:23). The LORD is well pleased when we approach Him in this manner.

The beginning of the Christian soldier's training, consequently, becomes a deep soul searching. We come boldly before the throne of grace yet, stand humbly petitioning Him. Our prayer training is not for the sake of self-importance or self-elevation but for the sake of the mission, His mission.

God's commission was for each of His children to reach the lost. We were recruited, as it were, when we obeyed the great plan of salvation in the book of Acts. We were enlisted when we chose to be born of the water and of the Spirit (John 3:3-7, Acts 2:38). We joined in the army of soldier prayer warriors around the globe.

As new babes in the Lord, we grew in the knowledge of God, and became acutely aware of the pressing need to pray. We began to understand that it's imperative to reach out to God for our spiritual survival. And now in front of us is the door of opportunity swinging wide to pray for the needs of others and their salvation.

Before we can effectively pray for others, we need to pray for our self as stated earlier. Praying scriptures for your self is like a walking plan; you need to do a little every day. Think of the novice who sets out to walk four miles per day to regain a healthy lifestyle.

If he hasn't walked outdoors for a year but lives a sedentary existence, he'd be foolish to try to tread the entire four miles. One must break it down in simple strides or you'll end up staggering home... the next day you'd be feeling muscles you never thought you had.

In walking, wisdom says to start with one or two miles until you can work your way up to the full distance. Your body will then have time to adjust and build up muscle tissue.

Sometimes the body will resist this new routine so your mind must be stronger that your flesh. My friend is a marathon runner, it is nothing for her to rise early and go for a 11-mile jog. If (tried) I trail with her, I couldn't jog two blocks because I'm not fit for the run.

Praying the Scriptures works the same way so pray a few verses in the beginning then work your spiritual muscles up to praying the full amount. You will eventually be led to your own personal prayer scriptures.

It's also smart to keep a prayer journal handy so you can keep an ongoing list of favorite verses to pray. It is a very rewarding journey. And, it is also a great way to memorize the Bible.

PUTTING IT INTO PRACTICE

Now in this section we will begin to pray for our self using various scriptures. "The Lord's Prayer" is a simple prayer pattern found in Matthew 6:9-10. Jesus was teaching His disciples simple principles in prayer. We are not to merely repeat the words over and over as a vain repetition, but understand what each segment means.

The following is a general prayer guide to help you get established in praying this portion of scripture. This is a good beginning until you create your own set of personal-prayer scriptures.

I've covered each section of the Lord's Prayer then added additional appropriate scriptures for further praying.

Principle   Scripture

PRAISE

(Vs. 9) *Our Father which art in heaven, Hallowed be thy name*

SUBMISSION

(Vs.10) *Thy kingdom come Thy will be done in earth, as it is in heaven*

PROVISION

(Vs.11) *Give us this day our daily bread*

FORGIVENESS

(Vs.12) *and forgive us our debts, as we forgive our debtors.*

PROTECTION

(Vs.13) *and lead us not into temptation, but deliver us from evil*

SOVERIEGNTY OF GOD

(Vs.13b) *for thine is the kingdom, and the power, and the glory, forever. Amen.*

Remember to put the scripture in the first person singular. All first-person notations here should be <u>underlined</u> and in SMALL CAPS. Let's begin with praising the Lord...

Scriptures for **Praise**

(Vs. 9) *Our Father which art in heaven, Hallowed be thy name*

1) *"Our Father which art in heaven, Hallowed be thy name"* <u>Matt. 6:9</u>
2) *"I will love thee, O LORD, my strength. The LORD is my rock, and my fortress, and my deliverer; my God, my strength, in whom I will trust; my buckler, and the horn of my salvation, and my high tower. I will call upon the LORD, who is worthy to be praised: so, shall I be saved from mine enemies."* <u>Psalms 18:1-3</u>
3) *"O God, thou art my God; early will I seek thee: my soul thirsteth for thee, my flesh longeth for thee in a dry and thirsty land, where no water is; to see thy power and thy glory, so as I have seen thee in the sanctuary. Because thy lovingkindness is better than life, my lips shall praise thee. Thus will I bless thee while I live: I will lift up my hands in thy name."* <u>Psalms 63:1-4</u>
4) *"I will bless the LORD at all times: his praise shall continually be in my mouth. My soul shall make her boast in the LORD: the humble shall hear thereof, and be glad. O magnify the LORD with me, and let us exalt*

his name together. I sought the LORD, and he heard me, and delivered me from all my fears." Psalms 34:1-4

5) "*I will praise thee, O LORD, with my whole heart; I will shew forth all thy marvelous works. I will be glad and rejoice in thee: I will sing praise to thy name, O thou most High.*" Psalms 9:1-2

Scriptures for **Submission**

(Vs.10) *Thy kingdom come Thy will be done in earth, as it is in heaven*

1) "*Thy kingdom come. Thy will be done in MY LIFE, as it is in heaven.*" Matt. 6:10
2) "*I present MYSELF as a living sacrifice, holy, acceptable unto God, which is MY reasonable service. And I WILL NOT BE conformed to this world: but I WILL BE transformed by the renewing* [renovation] *of MY mind, that I may prove what is that good, and acceptable, and perfect, will of God.*" Romans 12:1, 2
3) LORD, I PRAY TO BE "*...watch(ful) in all things* [clear-headed in all situations], *endure afflictions* [hardships, sufferings], *do the work of an evangelist, make full proof of MY ministry*" LORD, I PRAY TO [fully carry out the ministry God has given me, and devote myself completely to it]. " 2 Tim. 4:5
4) "*Let this mind be in you, which was also in Christ Jesus*" Phil 2:5 LORD, I PRAY THAT YOU BIND MY MIND TO YOUR MIND, MY WILL TO YOURS, MY EMOTIONS TO YOUR EMOTIONS, IN JESUS NAME.

5) LORD, I PRAY TO *"Walk in wisdom toward them that are without, redeeming the time. Let __MY__ speech be always with grace, seasoned with salt, that __I__ may know how __I__ ought to answer every man."* Col 4:5, 6

6) LORD, I PRAY TO *"sanctify the Lord God in __MY__ hearts: and be ready always to give an answer to every man that asketh __ME__ a reason of the hope that is in __ME__ with meekness and fear"* [that I would be gentle and have respect] 1 Peter 3:15

Scriptures for **Provision**
(Vs.11) *Give us this day our daily bread*

1) *"Give us this day our daily bread"* Matt 6:11
2) *"But my God shall supply all __MY__ need according to his riches in glory by Christ Jesus."* Phil. 4:19
3) *"__MAY I__ stand perfect and complete in all the will of God."* Col. 4:12
4) LORD, I PRAY THAT YOU COME AND *"build Your house through me that I labor not in vain."* Psalms 127:1
5) *"And let the beauty* [favor] *of the LORD our God be upon us: and establish thou the work of our hands upon us; yea, the work of our hands establish thou it."* Psa. 90:17
6) *"Forasmuch as an excellent spirit, and knowledge, and understanding, interpreting of dreams, and showing of hard sentences, and dissolving of doubts* [solve difficult problems], *were found in the same Daniel."* Daniel 5:12 LORD, I PRAY TO HAVE AN

EXCELLENT SPIRIT JUST AS YOUR SERVANT
DANIEL

7) *"Where there is no vision* [revelation], *the
people perish* [cast off restraint]: *but he that
keeps the law, happy is he."* Pro. 29:18 LORD,
I PRAY FOR REVELATION…OF YOUR WILL, AND
OF YOUR PLAN IN MY LIFE FOR TODAY. I ALSO
PRAY FOR REVELATION OF YOUR WORD, AND
OF YOUR SPIRIT THAT I MAY SHARE IT TO THE
PEOPLE/SINNERS SO THEY WILL NOT CAST-
OFF RESTRAINT; I ALSO PRAY FOR REVELATION
AND DIVINE GUIDANCE, THAT I MAY TELL IT TO
THE PEOPLE SO THAT THEY DON'T RUN WILD.

Scriptures for **Forgiveness**

(Vs.12) *and forgive us our debts, as we forgive our
debtors*

1) *"And forgive us our debts, as we forgive our
debtors."* Matt. 6:12 LORD, I FORGIVE THOSE
WHO HAVE OFFENDED ME AND HURT ME. AND, I
PRAY THAT IF THERE IS SOMEONE, I NEED TO
MAKE IT RIGHT WITH, SHOW ME THEIR FACE
AND I WILL GO TO THEM AND APOLOGIZE.

2) *"Create in me a clean heart, O God; and
renew a right spirit within me."* Psa. 51:10

3) [MAY] *"the blood of Jesus Christ his Son
cleanseth ME from all sin"* [or anything that
has made me unclean] 1 John 1:7 I PLEAD THE
BLOOD OF JESUS OVER MY LIFE TODAY

4) *"Keep MY tongue from evil, and MY lips from
speaking guile."* Psa. 34:13

5) *"YOUR grace is sufficient for ME: for YOUR
strength is made perfect in weakness. Most*

gladly therefore will I rather glory in my infirmities, that the power of Christ may rest upon me." 2 Cor. 12:9-10 *"Therefore I take pleasure in infirmities, in reproaches, in necessities, in persecutions, in distresses for Christ's sake: for when I am weak, then am I strong."*

6) *"A rash speaker is like piercings of a sword, and the tongue of the wise is healing."* Proverbs 12:18 (YLT) LORD, HELP MY LIPS BRING FORTH HEALING AND HELP ME NOT TO SPEAK LIKE THE PIERCINGS OF A SWORD

Scriptures for

Protection and Deliverance

(Vs.13) *and lead us not into temptation, but deliver us from evil*

1) *"And lead ME not into temptation, but deliver ME from evil"* Matt. 6:13

2) (*Prayer of Jabez*) *"Oh that thou wouldest bless me indeed, and enlarge my coast, and that thine hand might be with me, and that thou wouldest keep me from evil, that it may not grieve me! And God granted him that which he requested."* 1 Chr. 4:10

3) *"There hath no temptation taken you but such as is common to man: but God is faithful, who will not suffer* (allow) *ME to be tempted above that I AM able; but will with the temptation also make a way to escape, that I MAY be able to bear it."* 1 Cor. 10:13

4) *"The LORD will perfect that which concerneth me* [work out His plans and purpose for my life]*: thy mercy, O LORD, endureth forever: forsake not the works of thine own hands."* Psa. 138:8

5) *"Thy gentleness hath made me great thy gentleness hath made me great."* Psa. 18:35 LORD, I PRAY THAT YOU MAKE YOUR SPIRIT OF GENTLENESS GREAT IN ME

6) *"Being confident of this very thing, that he who has begun a good work in <u>ME</u> will perform it until the day of Jesus Christ"* Phil 1:6

7) *"Let no corrupt communication proceed out of <u>MY</u> mouth, but that which is good to the use of edifying, that it may minister grace unto the hearers. And,* I PRAY THAT I *grieve not the Holy Spirit of God, whereby <u>I AM</u> sealed unto the day of redemption.* LORD, I PRAY THAT I WOULD *Let all bitterness, and wrath, and anger, and clamor, and evil speaking, be put away from <u>ME</u>, with all malice: And <u>THAT I WOULD BE</u> kind one to another, tenderhearted, forgiving one another, even as God for Christ's sake hath forgiven <u>ME</u>."* Eph. 4:29-32

8) LORD, I PRAY THAT I WOULD *"Talk no more so exceeding proudly; let not arrogancy come out of <u>MY</u> mouth: for the LORD is a God of knowledge, and by him actions are weighed."* 1 Sam 2:3

9) LORD, I PRAY THAT I WOULD *"Set <u>MY</u> affection on things above, not on things on the earth. For <u>I AM</u> are dead, and <u>MY</u> life is hid with Christ in God."* Col. 3:2- 3

Scriptures for

Declaring the Sovereignty of God

(Vs.13b) *For thine is the kingdom, and the power, and the glory, forever. Amen*

1) *"For thine is the kingdom, and the power, and the glory, forever. Amen."* Matt. 6:13b
2) *"Now unto the King eternal, immortal, invisible, the only wise God, be honor and glory forever and ever. Amen."* 1 Timothy 1:17
3) *"Let God arise, let his enemies be scattered: let them also that hate him flee before him."* Psalms 68:1 LORD I PRAY THAT THE POWER OF GOD RISE IN MY LIFE TODAY
4) *"Now unto him that is able to do exceeding abundantly above all that we ask or think, according to the power that worketh in us, unto him be glory in the church by Christ Jesus throughout all ages, world without end. Amen."* Ephesians 3:20-21
5) *"One Lord, one faith, one baptism, One God and Father of all, who is above all, and through all, and in you all."* Ephesians 4:5-6
6) *"Hear, O Israel: The LORD our God is one LORD: and I shall love the LORD MY God with all MY heart, and with all MY soul, and with all MY might."* Deut. 6:4-5

Scriptures for

Christian Character Growth and Development

1) *"Be careful for nothing; but in everything by prayer and supplication with thanksgiving let your requests be made known unto God. And the peace of God, which passeth all understanding, shall keep your hearts and minds through Christ Jesus."* Phil 4:6-7 LORD, HELP ME TO REMEMBER TO PRAY ABOUT EVERYTHING AND NOT TO TRY TO FIGURE THINGS OUT ON MY OWN

2) *"... God hath called us to peace"* 1 Cor. 7:15 YOU HAVE CALL ME TO HAVE PEACE OF GOD IN MY LIFE

3) LORD, I PRAY THAT NO *"root of bitterness springing up trouble ME, and thereby be defiled."* Hebrews 12:15

1) *"If any of you lack wisdom, let him ask of God, that giveth to all men* [generously and without reprimand] *and it shall be given him."* James 1:5 LORD, I PRAY FOR WISDOM TODAY

2) LORD, I PRAY TO BE *"Swift to hear, slow to speak, slow to wrath: For the wrath of man worketh not the righteousness of God."* James 1:19, 20

3) LORD, I PRAY TO *"...be clothed with humility: for God resisteth the proud, and giveth grace to the humble."* 1 Peter 5:5

4) LORD, I PRAY TO *"Talk no more so exceeding proudly; let not arrogancy come out of MY mouth: for the LORD is a God of knowledge, and by him actions are weighed."* First Samuel 2:3

5) LORD, I PRAY TO HAVE *"the fruit of the Spirit*(which) *is love, joy, peace, longsuffering, kindness, goodness,*

faithfulness, gentleness, self-control." Galatians 5:22-23, 25 LORD, HELP ME TO REALIZE THAT EVERYTHING I NEED TO SUCCEED IN YOU IS IN THE FRUIT OF THE SPIRIT. *"If we live in the Spirit, let us also walk in the Spirit."* LORD, HELP ME TO CONFORM TO VIRTUE AND PIETY AND LIVE A LIFE PLEASING TO YOU

6) LORD, I PRAY FOR *"the manifestation of the Spirit* [which] *is given to each one for the profit of all:* 1) *the word of wisdom* 2) *the word of knowledge* 3) *faith* 4) *gifts of healings,* 5) *the working of miracles,* 6) *prophecy,* 7) *discerning of spirits,* 8) *different kinds of tongues,* 9) *the interpretation of tongues."* 1 Cor. 12:7-10 LORD, I PRAY FOR ADMINISTRATION AND GIFTS OF THE SPIRIT TO BE IN OPERATION IN MY LIFE AND IN MY CHURCH

7) *"And beside this, giving all diligence,* LORD, I PRAY TO *add to <u>MY</u> faith virtue; and to virtue knowledge; and to knowledge temperance; and to temperance patience; and to patience godliness; and to godliness brotherly kindness; and to brotherly kindness charity."* 2 Peter 1:5

8) LORD, I PRAY THAT *"Whatsoever things are true, honest, just, pure, lovely, whatsoever things are of good report; if there be any virtue, and if there be any praise,* THAT I WOULD *think on these things."* Phil. 4:8 IN JESUS NAME

THANK YOU LORD FOR HEARING MY PRAYERS TODAY, I PRAY ALL OF THIS TO YOU IN JESUS NAME. AMEN!

(<u>NOTE:</u> *You will pray to put on The Armor of God in the next chapter (Eph. 6:11-18).*

The Sword & The Sickle

*Be strong in the Lord, and
In the power of his might
Ephesians 6:10*

Chapter THREE
MIGHTY THRU GOD

PRAYING TO PUT ON THE ARMOR OF GOD

Spiritual warfare is like setting up a campsite. Before you settle down to make camp, you must clean the area free from rocks, twigs, and debris. The ground must not only be swept but also leveled so that your shelter will sit evenly.

After this is done, you will be ready to pitch your tent and take up occupancy. We too, need to get rid of any debris that has fallen on us to break our concentration. It is essential to sweep the area of our mind, as it were, to set up our spiritual tent.

This clearing of your mind will de-clutter the path to get a straight shot at the devil (*and his menacing cohorts*). We do this by praying these scriptures:

The Sword & The Sickle

LORD, I PRAY THAT YOU *"may give unto ME the spirit of wisdom and revelation in the knowledge of YOU: I PRAY THAT the eyes of MY understanding being enlightened; that I may know what is the hope of YOUR calling, and what the riches of the glory of YOUR inheritance in the saints, And what is the exceeding greatness of YOUR power to us-ward who believe, according to the working of YOUR mighty power, Which YOU wrought in Christ, when he raised him from the dead, and set him at his own right hand in the heavenly places"* Eph. 1:17-20

LORD, I PRAY THAT YOU *" would grant ME, according to the riches of YOUR glory, to be strengthened with might by YOUR Spirit in the inner man; That Christ may dwell in MY hearts by faith; that I, being rooted and grounded in love, May be able to comprehend with all saints what is the breadth, and length, and depth, and height; And to know the love of Christ, which passeth knowledge, that I might be filled with all the fullness of God. Now unto YOU that is able to do exceeding abundantly above all that we ask or think, according to the power that worketh in us"* Eph. 3:16-21

LORD, I PRAY THAT I WOULD *"be filled with the knowledge of YOUR will in all wisdom and spiritual understanding; That I might walk worthy of the Lord unto all pleasing, being fruitful in every good work, and increasing in the knowledge of God; Strengthened with all might, according to YOUR glorious power, unto all patience and longsuffering with joyfulness; Giving thanks unto the Father, which hath made us meet to be partakers of the inheritance of the saints in light"* Col. 1:9-12 Amen!

PRAYING THE ARMOR OF GOD

Thankfully, God has equipped His people with the Holy Ghost so that we don't have to fight the battle alone. He has supplied us with the full Armor of God. This protective covering is not just meager pieces of equipment that we haphazardly slap on.

God's Armor like a winter jacket fits snuggly around our spiritual man making us *"strong in the Lord and in the power of His might"* (Eph. 6:10). The Lord said He gave us *"power to tread upon serpents and scorpions"* (Luke 10:19). This power is better rendered in the original Greek as "authority."

If we don't use the authority God gave us to ward off evil spirits, they will have their free reign to build strongholds then take up residency in our lives.

It is interesting to note in First Samuel 13:22, the Bible declares that on the day of battle (with the children of Israel), *"not one sword or spear could be found among all the men who were with Saul and Jonathan."*

One wonders why they didn't use the confiscated weapons they obtained after the battle with the Philistines. Or why didn't King Saul arm his men with the spoils of the Ammonites? Was it that he lacked foresight to provide his men with the instruments of war so readily available?

There was no sword, no spear, nor javelin. It's no wonder his men scattered in dismay. The fledgling king Saul only set his troops up for failure. By this example we learn that effective leaders must project ahead in order to win the battle. The General in command must assess his surroundings, calculate needed supplies, and implement a plan of attack.

Our Lord Jesus is the very antithesis of this ancient king. He has provided all the equipment necessary to win every conflict. He has set up His Church to win against opposing forces. The fiercest attacks can be thwarted when we are clad with the **full Armor of God.**

Unlike the fruit of Spirit which is a byproduct of one receiving the Holy Ghost, the Armor of God must *literally* be put on by the believer himself. The Bible declares that we must *"Put on the whole armor of God, that you may be able to stand against the wiles of the devil"* (Eph. 6:11).

The underlined portion of the following scripture points out that success comes only when we use what God has provided for us as Christian soldiers. It then becomes our duty to be heavily armed with these weapons.

Paul reminds us in Second Corinthians 10:3, ***"For though we walk in the flesh, we do not war after the flesh: (For the weapons of our warfare are not carnal, but mighty through God to the pulling down of strongholds).***

This scripture is better rendered, *"The weapons we fight with are not the weapons of the world. On the contrary, they have divine power to demolish strongholds"* (NIV). This tells us that physical force is not the method we use against the schemes of the enemy or to spread the gospel.

In witnessing we are GENTLE, but in prayer, We are DEMONSTRATIVE
(Matthew 11:12)

The apostle Peter warned us to ***"Be sober, be vigilant; because your adversary the devil, as a roaring lion, walks about, seeking whom he may devour"*** (1 Peter 5:8). We must diligently be on watch to prevent the devil from devouring our soul, or the souls of our lost loved ones. And because the Bible gives us ample warning of such attacks, we must be ready to put him on the defense...or as they say in 21st century colloquialism, *"send him packing."*

It's in the adversary's nature to destroy whomsoever he may. He will make every attempt he gets. Like a reckoning ball, he maneuvers his little machine to destroy every bit of spiritual structure the Lord has built inside of you. We must protect ourselves from his blows and learn how to put him on the run.

A vigilant sober-minded soldier of Cross will neither be drunk with the cares of this life nor negligent in the fortifying of his spiritual inner-man. Sitting around idle and prayer less will not help us stay strong in the heat of the battle.

On the contrary, we'll be flustered, weakened, and run away. However, if we are prepared, we will be alert enough to prevent the enemy from breaking in and stealing our victories.

Unfortunately, some believers just meander around and do nothing when the battle rages; they close their eyes and hope not to see what is confronting them. Pitifully, they allow themselves to be lulled to sleep. Or, they just talk about it but not pray about it—this leads to the dog-chasing-its-tail mentality.

God's prayer warrior, just as a security guard who keeps an observant eye on the surveillance cameras, must stand at attention waiting for the Spirit's call. For they know they must be on the lookout as the watchman's duty is to keep awake and peruse cautiously for any lurking suspects.

All the while, the enemy's assaults try to steer us off the straight and narrow path of eternal life. His wiles are cheap attempts to lure us into defeat. His cunning devises bombard us with a barrage of distractions to get our mind off God and separate us from His presence.

God's soldiers must realize that old slough foot uses deceitful tactics to draw us ever so cleverly into a snare. The devil does not carry out an open onslaught nor challenge us face to face (though he may); he creeps in covertly with a disguise making his advances in darkness.

He is an invisible adversary moving ever so slyly and stealthily pouncing on the credulous soul with ambushes. He uses the alluring aspects that seem so harmless. His enticing pleasures are to catch one's eye to lead us into carnal indulgences until we've gone so far, we cannot retreat. His noise is deafening as so to impair us to hear the voice of the Lord.

Therefore, it's vital to avoid any stumbling blocks that hinder us from not putting on the full Armor of God. And, because our foes are numerous and forceful, and unless we are clothed with this divine protection, victory will be virtually impossible or at best, short lived.

Hence, to be a successful prayer warrior one must first **put on the full Armor of God** not just one piece here or one piece there. The unlearned believer will think that the helmet of salvation is all you need. Another babe in Christ may say "I witness to my family and friends, that's all I'm required to do." No, we need the total and complete set of God's protection. For it is only then we are sure to obtain our victories.

The Armor of God is not something that God Himself wears but what He provides for His children to put on. Obedience is imperative. Your conquests and spiritual victories will be gained by the force of the spoken quoted Word of God. Its **Living Mighty Power** will bring remarkable changes.

Let's look at the pieces of the ancient Roman soldier's armor mentioned in Ephesians 6:13-17.

BELT	**BREASTPLATE**
SANDALS	**HELMET**
SHIELD	**SWORD**

1) The **Belt** was made from leather, studded with metal plates. It protected the abdominal area of the soldier. Paul instructed us to have our *"loins girt about with truth"* (Eph. 6:14). It's also called **the belt of truth** which is buckled snugly around your waist.

Our love for the Truth, full Truth, all Truth, nothing but the Truth, will surround us like a belt around our waist. This belt which protected the reproductive part of the warrior also carried his sword. Loving the Truth of God's Word will give us the durability to proliferate the gospel of Jesus Christ (2 Thess. 2:10).

2) The **Breastplate of** [God's] **Righteousness** guards and protects us from punctures to vital areas of the chest. Our heart needs to be always safeguarded from harmful things that can pierce deep inside us. The breastplate of righteousness (right living) will keep a watch on our heart and soul. Its purpose is to keep our hearts from doing hurt, and getting hurt.

3) The **Sandals** [shoes] of readiness are to be worn to serve the gospel of Peace to hungry souls. *"And your feet shod with the preparation of the gospel of peace."* Peace is a calling. For God calls us to Peace, be at peace and walk in Peace (1 Cor. 7:15).

4) The **Shield** of faith is the moveable piece of the armor to repel the fiery darts of the devil. Make no mistake, darts will be fired. In the ancient days, fiery darts were used to burn down any standing structures. The enemy will launch his burning darts at you.

One translation render darts as *"burning missiles."* Sometimes thoughts come to our mind and burn in us and we can't seem to shake it. The fiery darts of doubt, scorching hurts or blazing deceit will try to burn down any walls of faith you might have.

The devil's goal is to destroy any spiritual structure that you have. He will (if you let him) try to set your Christian foundation (i.e., faith, hope, and trust in the Lord) on fire. But don't let his fire burn inside, extinguish it soon as possible. Lift the shield of faith and smother the embers before they spread.

The springs of Living water within us which is the Holy Ghost residing in our soul, can quench any fiery dart hurled our way. So, remember dig deep into the wells of salvation and put his fire out.

5) The **Helmet of Salvation** covers our thoughts and soothes our doubts. Baptism in Jesus Name and receiving the Holy Ghost with the evidence of speaking in tongues (Acts 2:38), and walking in the newness of life will ensure us to eternal life. The helmet of salvation will cover our mind with the blood of Jesus Christ.

Finally,

6) The **Sword of the Spirit** Learn to swing the Great Living Sword by speaking, quoting, declaring the Word of God in the Name of Jesus. It will make you victorious!

Note: The only sword Jesus had was the one in His mouth. We too, must keep the Word of God in our mouth and pray it out loud. Pray it often, never let it depart. The quoted Word of God is quicker and more powerful than lightning. You only need to try it and experience its results.

Praying this passage of scripture is how to **put on the full Armor of God.** We will then be prepared to fight the enemy.

LET'S BEGIN TO PRAY THESE SCRIPTURES (Ephesians 6:10-20):

LORD, I PRAY IN THE NAME OF JESUS TO *"be strong in the Lord, and in the power of his might. I* PRAY TO *put on the whole armor of God, that I may be able to stand against the wiles of the devil. For I wrestle not against flesh and blood, but against principalities, against powers, against the rulers of the darkness of this world, against spiritual wickedness in high places.*

Wherefore I take unto MYSELF the whole armor of God that I may be able to withstand in the evil day, and having done all, to stand. I stand therefore, having MY loins girt about with truth, and having on the breastplate of righteousness; and MY feet shod with the preparation of the gospel of peace;

Above all, I TAKE the shield of faith, wherewith I shall be able to quench all the fiery darts of the wicked. And I take the helmet of salvation, and the sword of the Spirit, which is the word of God: I WILL PRAY always with all prayer and supplication in the Spirit, and watching thereunto with all perseverance and supplication for all saints;

And for me, that utterance may be given unto me, that I may open my mouth boldly, to make known the mystery of the gospel, for which I am an ambassador in bonds: that therein I may speak boldly, as I ought to speak."

In Jesus Name I pray!

The Sword & The Sickle

Now, don't you just feel better already?

❧

For the word of God is quick,
And powerful, and sharper than any two edged sword,
Piercing even to the dividing asunder of soul and spirit, and of the
joints and marrow, and is a discerner of the thoughts
And intents of the heart
Hebrews 4:12

Chapter FOUR
Dual Nature of Prayer

Hurling the Sword & the Sickle

Some churches in the past have practiced the concept of binding and loosing spirits. This principle is found in Matthew 18:18 when Jesus said, *"Verily I say unto you, whatsoever ye shall bind on earth shall be bound in heaven: and whatsoever ye shall loose on earth shall be loosed in heaven."* Thankfully, many prayer warriors are acquainted to this effective way of praying.

This book will not focus on that dynamic axiom because there are excellent books that cover the subject in details.

The best I have ever read, and used for years is called, **"Strongman's His Name, What's His Game, Volume I & II** written by Drs. Jerry & Carol Robeson (*still available in bookstores*).

Some of the mentioned strongholds are: *familiar spirits, spirits of divination, jealousy, lying, haughtiness heaviness, whoredoms, infirmity, bondage, fear, anti-christ,* and *death.* There are more spirits which the book explains in details.

The Robesons counteract each wicked spirit with losing the Holy Ghost, Love of God, Spirit of Truth, and other attributes of God. Here is a recommended list of books that I enjoyed through the years:

- **Spiritual Warfare**—Judy Doughty
- **How to Conduct Spiritual Warfare**—Mary Garrison
- **Prayers that Prevail**—Richards & Hildebrand
- **Breaking Strongholds: Setting Captives Free**—Tom White
- **A Treasury of Prayer**—E.M. Bounds & Ravenhill
- **The Weapon of Prayer**—E.M. Bounds
- **The Secret of Believing Prayer**—Andrew Murray
- **Praying the Scriptures**—Judson Cornwall
- **A Woman's Guide to Spiritual Warfare**—Sherrer & Garlock
- **Supernatural Power**—Dr. James McKeever
- **The Believer's Authority**—Kenneth Hagin
- **Possessing the Gates of the Enemy**—Cindy Jacobs
- **Breaking Strongholds in Your City**—edited by C. Peter Wagner
- **The Prayer Journey**—Fredi Trammell
- **Praying the Word Effectively**—compiled by Linda Gleason

The Word of God is a two-edged sword that cuts in two directions. One penetrates deep into the heart of the inner man to sever unwanted mind-sets, and the other cuts into the etheric world of darkness to destroy the schemes of the devil.

The ancient sickle had serrated edges like our kitchen knives that were used for cutting the grain. We will use our harvest scriptures to cut the field of souls that are ripe in our city.

The past two chapters have been about scripture prayers to prepare for battle, now we are ready to declare God's promise for souls.

First scripture we pray is the Lord's Prayer request:

1) Matt 9:37-38 *"The harvest truly is plenteous, but the labourers are few; I pray* THAT *therefore the Lord of the harvest, that he will send forth labourers into his harvest"* AND INTO MY CITY OF <u>(fill in blank).</u>

2) John 4:35-38 *"Say not ye, There are yet four months, and then cometh harvest? Behold, I say unto you, Lift up your eyes, and look on the fields; for they are white already to harvest. And he that reapeth receiveth wages, and gathereth fruit unto life eternal: that both he that soweth and he that reapeth may rejoice together. And herein is that saying true, one soweth, and another reapeth. I sent you to reap that whereon ye bestowed no labour: other men laboured, and ye are entered into their labours."* FATHER, I PRAY THAT YOUR CHURCH WOULD NOT SAY THAT THERE IS FOUR MONTHS UNTIL HARVEST, BUT I PRAY THAT THEY WOULD LIFT UP THEIR EYES AND LOOK ON THE FIELDS FOR THEY ARE WHITE ALREADY TO HARVEST...SEND US TO REAP WHERE WE BESTOWED NO LABOR BUT HAVE ENTERED INTO THEIR LABORS.

3) ISA 6:8 *"I heard the voice of the Lord, saying, whom shall I send, and who will go for us?* LORD LET OUR CHURCH SAY, *Here* WE ARE; *send* US.*"*

4) Jeremiah 51:33 *"For thus saith the LORD of hosts, the God of Israel; the daughter of Babylon is like a threshing floor, it is time to thresh her: yet a little while, and the time of her harvest shall come."* LORD, MAKE MY CITY OF <u>(fill in blank)</u> THRESHING FLOOR SO THAT THE TIME OF HER HARVEST WILL COME NOW, TODAY! • thresh a) *To beat out grain from (wheat stalks, etc.) by treading, striking with a flail, etc. b) To go repeatedly, as in discussion or argument*

5) Joel 3:13 *"Put ye in the sickle, for the harvest is ripe"* LORD, PUT SICKLES IN THE HANDS OF YOUR PEOPLE THAT WE MAY REAP THE HARVEST THAT IS RIPE THROUGHOUT THIS AREA <u>(NAME YOUR CITY)</u>

6) Psalm 2:8 *"Ask of me, and I shall give thee the heathen for thine inheritance, and the uttermost parts of the earth for thy possession"* LORD YOU SAID TO ASK AND WE'RE ASKING IN THE NAME OF JESUS THAT YOU WOULD GIVE US THIS CITY FOR OUR POSSESSION, GIVE US SOULS TO BE SAVED BY YOU.

7) Isaiah 45:11 *"Thus saith the LORD, the Holy One of Israel, and his Maker, Ask me of things to come concerning my sons, and concerning the work of my hands command ye me"* LORD, WE COMMAND IT TO BE SO, THAT YOU WOULD GO AND WORK IN THESE PEOPLE'S LIVES WHO YOU ARE DEALING WITH TO COME AND SERVE YOU IN THIS CHURCH.

8) Isa 43:13 *"Yea, before the day was I am he; and there is none that can deliver out of my hand; I will work, and who shall let* it?"* LORD, WE WILL LET YOU AND WE WILL NOT HINDER THE WORK THAT YOU ARE DOING IN OUR CITY.

9) Psalm 119:126 *"It is time for thee, LORD, to work"* LORD, HEAR OUR PRAYER AND WORK FOR US AND WORK THROUGH US AND LET YOUR SPIRIT DRAW SINNERS TO YOU.

10) Psalms 22: 27-28 *"All the ends of the world shall remember and turn unto the LORD: and all the kindreds of the nations shall worship before thee. For the kingdom is the LORD's: and he is the governor among the nations"* LORD, LET US FIND THOSE OF ALL NATIONS WHO ARE READY TO WORSHIP YOU.

11) Daniel 7:14 *"And there was given him dominion, and glory, and a kingdom, that all people, nations, and languages, should serve him: his dominion is an everlasting dominion, which shall not pass away, and his kingdom that which shall not be destroyed."* LORD, WE STAND ON THESE PROMISES THAT THERE IS A PEOPLE IN (NAME YOUR city) THAT WILL SERVE YOU.

12) John 15:16 *"Ye have not chosen me, but I have chosen you, and ordained you, that ye should go and bring forth fruit, and that your fruit should remain: that whatsoever ye shall ask of the Father in my name, he may give it you."* LORD, WE PRAY FOR THOSE IN THIS CITY THAT

YOU'VE CHOSEN AND ORDAINED TO COME AND BRING FORTH FRUIT.

13) Acts 28:28 *"Be it known therefore unto you, that the salvation of God is sent unto the Gentiles, and that they will hear it."* LORD, LEAD US TO THOSE WHO WILL HEAR THIS GOSPEL AND GIVE THEIR LIFE TO YOU.

14) Joel 3:9 *"Proclaim, ye this among the Gentiles; Prepare war, wake up the mighty men, let all the men of war draw near; let them come up"* LORD, LEAD THE MIGHTY MEN OF OUR CHURCH TO DRAW NEAR AND PREPARE FOR WAR AGAINST THE ENEMY OF OUR SOULS, GIVE THEM STRENGTH TO COME UP AND FIGHT.

15) Mark 16:20 *"And they went forth, and preached everywhere, the Lord working with them, and confirming the word with signs following. Amen."* LORD, HELP US TO GO FORTH AND PREACH EVERYWHERE [AS YOU LEAD] AND WORK WITH US AND CONFIRM YOUR WORD WITH SIGNS FOLLOWING EACH OF US.

Don't stop here but go to the next chapter to keep your momentum and the Spirit of prayer flowing.

The Sword & The Sickle

Then you shall rise from the ambush,
And seize the city:
For the LORD your God
Will deliver it into your hand
Joshua 8:7

Chapter FIVE

Rejoice
For God Has Given Us This City

After much prayer you'll see that people will be persuaded to follow the Lord and find their way back to God. We are the vessels simply carrying the good news of the Gospel to them. We can now declare the promises of the Lord given to us in His word.

Let's declare God's promises back to Him and say:

16) Isa 55:11 *" So shall <u>YOUR</u> word be that goeth forth out of <u>OUR</u> mouth: it shall not return unto <u>YOU</u> void, but it shall accomplish that which <u>YOU</u> please, and it shall prosper in the thing where to <u>YOU</u> sent it.*

17) Jeremiah 5:14 *"Wherefore thus saith the LORD God of hosts, Because ye speak this word, behold, I will make my words in thy mouth fire, and this people wood, and it shall devour them"* THANK YOU LORD, WE STAND ON THESE

PROMISES THAT THERE YOU WILL CAUSE THE PEOPLE WE WITNESS TO TODAY WILL FEEL A BURNING IN THEIR HEART TO KNOW YOU MORE.

18) Acts 28:28 *"Be it known therefore unto you, that the salvation of God is sent unto the Gentiles, and that they will hear it"* THANK YOU LORD THAT OUR PRAYERS ARE NOT IN VAIN BUT THE PEOPLE YOU SEND US TO WILL HEAR IT.

19) Isaiah 64:7 *"And there is none that calleth upon thy name that stirreth up himself to take hold of thee: for thou hast hid thy face from us, and hast consumed us, because of our iniquities."* THANK YOU, LORD, THAT EVEN NOW THERE IS A STIRRING IN THE HEARTS OF MEN AND WOMEN TO TAKE HOLD OF YOU AND LEARN OF YOU.

20) Isaiah 45:3 *"And I will give thee the treasures of darkness, and hidden riches of secret places, that thou mayest know that I, the LORD, which call thee by thy name, am the God of Israel."* THANK YOU, LORD, THAT YOU HAVE PROMISED US TO GIVE THIS TREASURE OF SOULS.

21) Psalms 2:8 *"Ask of me, and I shall give thee the heathen for thine inheritance, and the uttermost parts of the earth for thy possession."* THANK YOU, LORD, THAT WE MAY ASK OF YOU AND YOU WILL GIVE US THIS GREAT HARVEST OF SOULS.

22) Psalms 22: 27 *"All the ends of the world shall remember and turn unto the LORD: and all the kindreds of the nations shall worship before thee."* THANK YOU, LORD, THAT WE HAVE THIS PROMISE THAT OUR PRAYERS ARE NOT IN VAIN BUT THAT ALL TYPES OF PEOPLE SHALL BE SAVED AS WE CRY OUT FOR THEIR SOUL.

23) Psalm 119:126 *"It is time for thee, LORD, to work: for they have made void thy law."* THIS IS YOUR TIME TO WORK LORD AND TO DO A WORK THROUGH US AMEN.

24) Hosea 6:3 *"Then shall we know, if we follow on to know the LORD: his going forth is prepared as the morning; and he shall come unto us as the rain, as the latter and former rain unto the earth."* LORD, WE ARE SO GRATEFUL THAT WE HAVE THIS PROMISE TO FOLLOW YOU AND YOU'LL BE WITH US IN ALL WE DO FOR YOUR KINGDOM.

Praise the LORD we have a promise of a harvest souls.

The Sword & The Sickle

"... Men of stature, shall come over unto thee,
And they shall be thine: they shall come after thee;
In chains they shall come over, and they shall fall
Down unto thee, they shall make supplication unto thee,
saying, surely God is in thee; and there is none else;
There is no [other] God."
Isaiah 45:14

Chapter SIX

Collecting the Spoils from Warfare

Many of the following testimonies were brought by the hand of God when I prayed against spirits and bound the strongman related to the issue. All the glory goes to our great and awesome God.

In some cases, I felt to anoint buildings, houses, or places which the wickedness presided. Just to note: there is nothing in Scripture that commands or even suggests that we should anoint with oil similar places today, but neither is there anything to forbid it. So, I just did it by faith. And, it worked.

First, here is a little history on anointing oil.

In a nutshell, anointing oil is mentioned 20 times in Scripture. It was used in the Old Testament for pouring on the head of the high priest and his descendants and sprinkling the tabernacle and its furnishings to mark them as holy and set apart to the Lord (Exodus 25:6; Leviticus 8:30; Numbers 4:16).

The first mention of someone anointing something was in Genesis 28:18, *"And Jacob rose up early in the morning, and took the stone that he had put for his pillows, and set it up for a pillar, and <u>poured oil upon the top of it.</u>"* The editors of the *Ryrie Study Bible* comment that by pouring this anointing oil, Jacob "consecrated" the pillar, thereby rendering it an altar holy unto God.

To be "anointed" is, among other things, to be made sacred (consecrated); to be set apart and dedicated to serve God. Oil is often used as a symbol for the Holy Ghost in the Bible as in the Parable of the Wise and Foolish Virgins (Matthew 25:1-13).

Christians filled with the Holy Ghost are led into all truth. Thus, the Holy Ghost "anoints" us continually with His grace and comfort. We are anointed to accomplish His will.

Should Christians use anointing oil today? I do. That is what I did in many cases and God moved in an awesome way. Here is a baker's dozen of amazing testimonies (*yet there are more*). They are not in any chronologically order just as I remembered them. ENJOY!

Testimonies

ONE

There was a fortune teller/psychic on the corner of El Camino and Benton St in my home town in California. I used to have to drive by it to get to school and work. Her white house had a statue of a wizard on the front post of the porch.

Day after day I would drive by it. I began to feel vexed in my spirit at this person, presuming it was a woman. She was leading souls into witchcraft. So, I decided to make every effort to pray against the spirit of divination and familiar spirits. I would lose the Holy Ghost to chase her out of town and free the unknowing souls that would go to her for counsel.

One day I saw an old lady (*she looked like an Old Italian lady you see in pictures*) walking with a young man, perhaps it was her 40-year-old son. I said Lord don't let her continue in this wicked practice. Shut her down, close her shop. I continued to pray this way for weeks.

Then one day, I noticed the wizard was gone off the porch. Then in a month or so afterwards, the windows were boarded up. The house was empty. And finally, the house was bulldozed and now, it's an empty lot! **Praise God.**

TWO

This happen also in my town of Nashua, NH. I saw fortune teller/psychic house. I kept on rebuking this spirit and binding it and casting out of town. Sure enough, the business closed and the building is up for sale. It took a few years but she is gone for good. **Thank you, Jesus!**

THREE

Another time, I would shop at the Costco on Senter Road, San Jose, CA. The block before I'd get there was a pornography book store. In them days, we called it a "skin shop." That place just got to me, especially when I'd see cars parked in front of that store.

Those people hooked on that stuff needed deliverance. I began to pray and pray every time I went there to Costco. I'd bind the wicked spirits of whoredoms, bondage, perversion, and lust.

I prayed that God Almighty would shut that place down for good. Lo, to my amazement…that place burned to the ground and they built a shoe store in its place! **Oh hallelujah!**

FOUR

My pastor friend in Illinois asked me to come preach a revival for her. It was 1993 and I was a novice preacher but not a novice prayer warrior. In the meantime, she was having trouble with one of the saints in her church that caused big-time trouble.

This lady (*I believe her name was Wanda*) spread lies and stirred up so much dissention in the church; she caused a church split and put the pastor out. She changed the locks on the door of the church and cut the electricity off so we couldn't hold our revival.

This however, did not stop us from having church in the pastor's home. And so we did for three days. During this time, the prayer warrior in me was fired up to pray against this lying spirit and jealous spirit and witchcraft (*born out of rebellion*). I told the pastor I will go and anoint that lady's house at night when nobody was watching. *Oh my! Is there not a cause?*

So, I went on her bicycle to that lady's house when it was dark. To that, my pastor friend said if the lady catches me, she'd probably shoot me dead. That's when you must know angels are surrounding you and that God will protect you in the heat of the battle.

The night came, I went around that house and bushes I threw anointing oil on the rebel lady's house and cast out those spirits. Lo, and behold, she never did go and make it right with my pastor friend. Then almost one year later to the date, that lady took sick with cancer and died on the spot.

FIVE

On Saratoga Avenue in Santa Clara there is a place called Tinker's Damn. It was a gay bar that many would visit. When I was a teenager, I knew friends that would go in there.

After I got saved and learned how to pray, I saw the evil in that kind of place. Through the years my prayer partners and I would bind those wicked spirits that ruled over that place. It was disgusting just to think of what went on in there.

Every time I'd drive by, be sure I'd bind spirits and cast them out. Lo, and behold, the place closed January 2014. They sold the property and built all new stores. **Praise God!**

THEN　　　　　　**NOW**

SIX

Back in the days before internet was invented, and I was still living in California I'd on a few occasions see discarded books on the road. I believe the Holy Ghost prompted me to stop and see what it was. Sure enough, it was a pornography magazine somebody had thrown from a car. (*That lying devil*)

I thought wait a minute here; a young person could easily stumble upon it and take it home...Well, not on my watch.

I told the LORD the next time I see a book like that I will go and burn it and set the captive free. Lo and behold, a week goes by and I saw another one on the street.

I whipped my car around so fast and grabbed that filthy thing and drove to the nearest park. I poured anointing oil over it and SET IT ON FIRE! I prayed deliverance for the person who was trapped in this habit and prayed against the spirit of perversion, lust, and bondage. This happened a few times so the next time I'd be ready. I resorted to keep a lighter and oil in my car.

You may ask if this really had any effect. Well, all I know is that every time I burned books at a park, I would come home and on my telephone's answering machine there would be the grossest obscene phone call I've ever gotten (*he is a dirty devil*).

SEVEN

After the 1989 Loma Prieta earthquake in Santa Clara Valley, I heard that the people of Santa Cruz had to rebuild the town that got flattened. When they finished the new structures, there was talk that they were going to have a fire walk and dedicate it to Satan. The witches were thrilled. Santa Cruz is known to be a witches' haven.

Many people would speak of their boldness even to knock doors when they were going to have an animal sacrifice and invite people to it. It was common to see dead animals in the woods with their blood drained from them. It was known that the police department feared and would just leave them alone.

Knowing all of this, my spirit was vexed inside me. One day my friends and I decided to go to Santa Cruz for a day outing to the beach wharf. But when I got there, I felt a spirit of oppression hovering over that city like a thick fog.

As we were casually walking around looking at shops, we endeavored to pass out church tracks. I couldn't believe what I was looking at next: <u>a satanic ritual supply shop</u>. Shocked and vexed, I talked my friends who are great prayer warriors to go inside and wage war.

I said we must go in there and set those captives free. We were not just going to kindly anoint a dot of oil with our finger but we were going in to do spiritual battle. When we went into the shop, our hands were dripping with oil and we began to pray out loud over the blaring music.

We cried out in the name of Jesus and pleading the blood to set these people free. My friend said that God opened her eyes. When we stepped in through the door, she saw the demons backed away like a bowling ball hitting the pins.

We smeared oil on the countertops and on the walls and just about everywhere we could. The sales guy didn't see it coming (*I think he was spaced out on something*).

Pacific Street, Santa Cruz CA

We went into the back room where there was an area that sold all the pornographic books and Sadomasochism supplies...*ugh, disgusting*! It was horrible; God protected our eyes as we prayed to set the captives free. And that we did.

71

I never did go back to see if the shop closed. I only hope it did. When I tried to look it up on the Google, it deleted the words immediately. **Oh, Praise God!**

EIGHT

For nine and a half years my husband and I were over the new believers' classes. We were having great revival which we attribute it to the early Morning Prayer meetings at the church. It was during that time our church was engaged in a lot of spiritual warfare.

For example, one six-week revival with Rev. Earl Lee preaching brought in over 323 new souls. We had altar worker's cards with names and addresses. These people got the Holy Ghost and/or been baptized in Jesus Name.

During all this soul rush came some unwanted deviants. There was one lady who we were working with. She came faithfully to our Disciple's classes on Sunday mornings. Her name was Leslie; at least that is what she told us only to find out later not true.

She was always in my prayer circle during prayer time at church. I notice that when she'd pray, I couldn't think of a scripture to save my life. She was somehow jamming up my mental circuits.

As weeks went by, this woman started needing rides home to which I obliged. But on our ride home I noticed she would answer me before I even asked the question, I was planning on asking; pretty strange.

Then she would start making comments about the things of God (mostly church standards) and make snide remarks about them. I began to sense a spirit of hocus pocus going on. She invited me into her apartment. There was a HUGE picture of what she called her spirit guide. She had all kinds of New Age paraphernalia in her house.

How could this be she seemed so nice and supposedly got saved? We would let her play her harp in New Converts class and everyone was friendly to her.

All was fine until one day I made a mistake and accepted a book she "loaned" me. It was on the New AGE and their belief of Jesus Christ.

Lo, and behold, that night that woman astral projected into my bedroom and was trying to choke me to death. The spirit of fear was so great on me that it caused me to tremble. I couldn't quote one verse of Scripture to save my life.

There was a heavy battle going on. My husband woke up and tried to pray her off me. Though he couldn't see what was going on, I tried to speak but couldn't. This went on through the night until 4AM then the Holy Ghost spoke to me and said, "Get that book out of the house; this is how she entered in."

I muttered the words to my husband and he quickly threw that thing out the front door. When he did, immediately the spirit of fear and that "thing" left me. Wow, I was pretty shaken up in the morning and battle weary. The story doesn't end there.

I knew then she was a witch. Later we found out her name was Carol and wasn't married before, but a lesbian, and a Wiccan who already entered a blood covenant by slicing her wrists.

When I began to put all the pieces together, I started to watch her closely at church especially at altar call. I noticed while she was praying with women, I could see her rubbing their arms, backs and hugging a little too long.

She occasionally would attend our Thursday morning ladies Bible study. By then, my spirit began to get vexed. I finally said, "That did it devil, she is out of here."

I prayed "In the Name of Jesus, I plead the blood of Jesus. Satan, I rebuke you. If you bring this woman back to our church ONE MORE TIME, mark it down, and I will expose you for what this is. You have no right here, now leave in Jesus Name and don't come back."

You know, that woman NEVER DID come back to our church again.

Oh, look at the LORD and all He hath done!

NINE

We moved to the East Coast and finally settled in New Hampshire. We became the associate pastors at a church in Fitchburg MA. All was going well until the autumn time.

The person in the house across the street of the church decided to decorate for Halloween. Ugh! I mean, she did so to the maximum.

There was a giant headless horseman, demon figures, lights, and graveyard scenario with bloody figures. Gross! I thought, "Right across from the House of God?" We are a holy people and don't want to be slapped in the face with looking at that wickedness as we enter church.

So, when the next year came along and it was fall season, I went to praying. I decided there will be no show of demonic figures and costumes on my watch.

I walked across the street and poured oil over the sidewalk and prayed in Jesus Name. I commanded the devil leave this woman and said that there would be no Halloween decorations OF ANY KIND put out there.

And lo, and behold, she never did put ANYTHING out there on her lawn again. And that has been for the last six years! **To God be the Glory!**

TEN

We are now church planters in the city of Lowell, MA. The little building, we rented is in the projects. There is a bar (*they call it a café*) next door to our church near a parking lot. It's noisy and drunks coming and going; a pitiful sight. Upstairs from the bar is two apartments, at times I'd wonder if it could be a prostitution ring.

I was hoping to reach out to people there. As time went on, we continued to have service in our little church. One day I became vexed knowing people next door were being led astray by the spirit of bondage, alcohol, smoking whatever and perhaps, lust and corruption.

My mind was swirling with this. So, I grabbed the bottle of oil, left the church service, went outside, and headed for the bar. It was not open yet, so I poured oil in Jesus Name and smeared it on the door posts and claimed deliverance and freedom from bondage of these spirits. I asked the LORD to set these captives free.

Lo, and behold in a few months the bar closed. Then months later we learned that they sold the building.

Finally, we came to church and noticed that the whole building was bulldozed to the ground. **Wow, Look at the LORD!**

ELEVEN

It is our custom at the Lowell Church to do prayer walks. We were endeavoring to teach our new believers the art of prayer walking. We only walked a few square blocks to pray and pass out tracks.

This one Saturday we walked by a corner street where there were some Jehovah Witnesses standing on the corner with their literature. They didn't really seem to be doing much outreaching. We were friendly to them with the hope to "witness" to them the Truth of Jesus Name. The one man however was defensive and cold.

A few weeks went by and we did another prayer walk. And sure, enough there were the JWs standing under the Willow tree on the same corner with their literature. We just passed by.

I told our new convert, Robert, next time we are going to pray and anoint that place where they are standing. We are going to pray against their influence and propagation of falsehood. And that we did.

I instructed Robert to pour oil on the sidewalk where they were standing as I prayed in the Name of Jesus while my husband chatted with the JWs. I bound the spirit of error, antichrist, and lying spirits. We came against any allurement they might have. We said that spirit it had to go!

Lo, and behold the next few months when we had an opportunity to go do another prayer walk in that area, we noticed that the Willow tree had been cut down to the ground and the JWs were gone! **Oh my, Look at the LORD!**

TWELVE

Many times, I go home to visit my home church, family, and friends. And when I was growing up there was an X-rated movie theatre on the corner of Bascom and 280 Freeway (Burbank Theatre). My college was two blocks away.

Every time I'd drive by that place, I'd rebuke that foul spirit. One day when I was going to school, I began to feel that vexing in my spirit over that rotten place. I decided when I get a chance, I was going to anoint it in Jesus Name. I'd pray against the spirits of lust, perversion, bondage, and corruption, cast it out and send back to hell where it belonged.

Now, it came to me that if a go over there and somebody see me near the doors of the theatre that they might think that I was entering into that place to watch those disgusting movies.

So, I came up with a plan (*don't try this at home, folks*). I bought a kids squirt gun and filled it up with oil. I drove by that place thinking this will be my first drive by shooting. But the oil didn't reach far enough, so I got out of my car and walked (*quickly*) by the doors and shot the oil all over the doors and walls of the building. Then I tore out of there!

Finally, I went back to California to visit my family and friends. And after years of this place being open for the deviant's pleasure, I noticed that this place was boarded up and shut DOWN for business! **Oh Hallelujah! Glory to God!**

THIRTEEN

I cannot forget to tell you this one. In June 2015, my husband and I joined 200+ prayer warriors to meet and pray in Washington DC. The three-day prayer meeting was held at Rev. Ron Libby's church. Oh my, what a powerful demonstration of spiritual warfare that went on in that place.

On that Saturday we loaded into the buses. Before we headed to Wash DC, prayer warriors were divided into groups. The plan was that we were going to pray (quietly) and anoint (discreetly) the buildings we were assigned to.

I oversaw the Dept. of Health and Human Services. I was happy about that because they were indirectly responsible for all the millions of abortions that took place in our country. I was ready to go to war for the unborn babies.

We went to praying; binding spirits and asking God to put an end to the works of the devil. Now, I'm not saying that it was my group's prayer that was completely responsible for this victory but…

It was six weeks later that the news broke out about Planned Parenthood selling fetal parts. They were caught red-handed on tape. This put a stop to the funding...at least, for a short while.

To God be the Glory!!!

1 Corinthians 2:4, 5

"And my speech and my preaching was not with enticing words of man's wisdom, but in <u>demonstration of the Spirit and of power</u>: That your faith should not stand in the wisdom of men, but in the power of God."

The LORD asked Moses, "What's in thine hand?" Moses replied, "A rod." All he had was a Shepherd's stick; an instrument or tool that he used every day doing his work as a shepherd.

We too, must use what is in our hand. *What's in your hand, friend?* A Bible; this is what we need to use to get through everyday life. It's more than just "a good read" it's a workbook to use, and a manual and guide, so that we can live a victorious overcoming life.

Let me ask you, "What's in your hand?" What devil needs rebuking and smearing oil over? We have the Bible, we have the Blood, and we have the promise of God to be with us in our battles.......so, what's stopping you?

Got devils? We got the LORD...
And a little bit of anointing oil!

The Sword & The Sickle

O sing unto the LORD a new song;
For he hath done marvelous things:
Psalm 98:1

Chapter SEVEN

Praise Break

1) Psalms 103:1-5 *"Bless the LORD, O my soul: and all that is within me, bless his holy name. Bless the LORD, O my soul, and forget not all his benefits: Who forgiveth all thine iniquities; who healeth all thy diseases; Who redeemeth thy life from destruction; who crowneth thee with lovingkindness and tender mercies; who satisfieth thy mouth with good things; so that thy youth is renewed like the eagle's."*

2) Psalms 103:1-5 *"Praise ye the LORD. Sing unto the LORD a new song, and his praise in the congregation of saints. Let Israel rejoice in him that made him: let the children of Zion be joyful in their King. Let them praise his name in the dance: let them sing praises unto him with the tumbrel and harp. For the LORD taketh pleasure in his people: he will beautify the meek with salvation. Let the saints be joyful in glory: let them sing*

aloud upon their beds. Let the high praises of God be in their mouth, and a two-edged sword in their hand; to execute vengeance upon the heathen, and punishments upon the people; to bind their kings with chains, and their nobles with fetters of iron; to execute upon them the judgment written: this honour have all his saints. Praise ye the LORD."

3) Psalms 5:11 *"But let all those that put their trust in thee rejoice: let them ever shout for joy, because thou defendest them: let them also that love thy name be joyful in thee."*

4) Psalms 8:1-6 *"O LORD, our Lord, how excellent is thy name in all the earth! Who hast set thy glory above the heavens. Out of the mouth of babes and sucklings hast thou ordained strength because of thine enemies, that thou mightest still the enemy and the avenger. When I consider thy heavens, the work of thy fingers, the moon and the stars, which thou hast ordained; what is man, that thou art mindful of him? and the son of man, that thou visitest him? For thou hast made him a little lower than the angels, and hast crowned him with glory and honour. Thou madest him to have dominion over the works of thy hands; thou hast put all things under his feet:"*

5) Psalms 92:1-5 *"It is a good thing to give thanks unto the LORD, and to sing praises unto thy name, O Most High: to shew forth thy lovingkindness in the morning, and thy faithfulness every night, upon an instrument of ten strings, and upon the psaltery; upon the harp with a solemn sound. For thou, LORD, hast made me glad through thy work: I will triumph in the works of thy*

> hands. *O LORD, how great are thy works! And thy thoughts are very deep."*

6) Isaiah 12:1-6 *"And in that day thou shalt say, O LORD, I will praise thee: though thou wast angry with me, thine anger is turned away, and thou comfortedst me. Behold, God is my salvation; I will trust, and not be afraid: for the LORD JEHOVAH is my strength and my song; he also is become my salvation. Therefore with joy shall ye draw water out of the wells salvation. And in that day shall ye say, Praise the LORD, call upon his name, declare his doings among the people, make mention that his name is exalted. Sing unto the LORD; for he hath done excellent things: this is known in all the earth. Cry out and shout, thou inhabitant of Zion: for great is the Holy One of Israel in the midst of thee.*

7) Psalms 149 *Praise ye the LORD. Sing unto the LORD a new song, and his praise in the congregation of saints. Let Israel rejoice in him that made him: let the children of Zion be joyful in their King. Let them praise his name in the dance: let them sing praises unto him with the timbrel and harp. For the LORD taketh pleasure in his people: he will beautify the meek with salvation. Let the saints be joyful in glory: let them sing aloud upon their beds. Let the high praises of God be in their mouth, and a two-edged sword in their hand; to execute vengeance upon the heathen, and punishments upon the people; To bind their kings with chains, and their nobles with fetters of iron; To execute upon them the judgment written: this honour have all his saints. Praise ye the LORD.*

Selah!

The Sword & The Sickle

Made in the USA
Middletown, DE
24 October 2024